WHAT OTHERS ARE SAYING

"As a young university student I enrolled in a creative writing course for extra credit. My lecturer, who was generally incredibly encouraging of my work, noted that if my poems were ballets then the ballerinas would probably knock over the scenery or fall off the stage. This collection of poems is nothing like that. These heartfelt poems are rich and meaningful. The ballet that is this collection dances with abandon and leaps with the joy of the Creator. They are, quite simply, magnificent. Thank you Ana Lisa for producing a wonderful ballet of words and images that will stir the soul and make the heart soar. This book will be a welcome addition to any collection of inspirational Christian poetry."

PRINCIPAL DEFENCE FORCE CHAPLAIN,
CHAPLAIN LANCE LUKIN OSTJ, QHC.

"These entries reveal such depth and beauty, richness and insight. A fresh awareness of the presence of God in every season. Take your time to reflect, and be drawn closer to your Creator."

SHAREE HARKNESS, WORSHIP DIRECTOR,
MUSIC SPECIALIST TEACHER

"Songs in the night exposes the heart of a woman world weary from wrestling with God and with herself – yet one who also knows the joy and peace that come from collapsing in surrender in God's arms breathless and exhausted."

REV DIANE GILLIAM-WEEKS, EDITOR REFRESH
JOURNAL OF CONTEMPLATIVE SPIRITUALITY

Songs in the Night

— POETRY FOR THE SOUL —

Ana Lisa de Jong

BOOK PUBLISHING

Wellington, New Zealand

langbookpublishing.com

No part of this book may be reproduced, stored in a retrieval system, or transmitted by any means, electronic, mechanical, photocopying, recording, or otherwise without written permission from the author.

Copyright © Ana Lisa de Jong 2014. All rights reserved.

"The right of Ana Lisa de Jong to be identified as author of the Work has been asserted by her in accordance with the New Zealand Copyright Act 1994."

National Library of New Zealand Cataloguing-in-Publication Data

Lang Book Publishing Limited 2014

Scripture quotations are taken from THE HOLY BIBLE, NEW INTERNATIONAL VERSION®, NIV® Copyright © 1973, 1978, 1984, 2011 by Biblica, Inc.® Used by permission. All rights reserved worldwide.

978-0-9941151-6-4 – Paperback
978-0-9941151-7-1 – eBook

Published in New Zealand

*To all those who have
given me reason to write.
Thank you.*

Contents

Foreword 9
Introduction 11
Seasons 13

PART 1: SONGS IN THE NIGHT

There is a Time 16
The Tender Places 19
Sanctification 21
Brother, Sister 23
Missing You 26
Loss 28
God is in a Stone 30
Black and Blue 32
Heartbroken 35
Don't Go Back 38
The Bright Side 40
Songs in the Night 42

PART 2: ODE TO THE DAWN

To Remember 46
Joy 48
Hope 50
Love Knocks 52
Help me to See 54
My Lord 57

Because You Love me 60
I Look for You 63
I Turn to You 66
Where I Stand 68
Grace 71
He's Calling 75
Your Table 78
The Edge 81

PART 3: JOY IN THE MORNING

Limitless Hope 84
To the Sun 87
The Way of the Cross 89
Christmas Morning 91
No Need 94
To Know You 96
There is an Ocean 99
Something to Show You 103
The Way 105
God in Me 107
Learning of Love 110
God's Guidance 113
What Moves You? 115
Surrounded by Love 117
I See You 120
He Loves Us 122
Life – As a Gift 125
What We Believe 128
Time 131
Photo Appendix 134

Foreword

When I started my journey towards God, He revealed Himself to me through a number of ways, which at the time I didn't always recognize. He revealed Himself to me through biblical preaching. I saw Him through the beauty of creation, the starry universe above, the beauty of the mountains and the rivers below, the sunsets and the sunrises. I knew then that my life and the world around me didn't happen by chance.

God also revealed Himself to me through people's lives, and it was here that I truly started to understand the impact this God can have on human beings. For these people were like windows for me to look through, to see into the heart of God.

I met Ana Lisa about eleven years ago and knew straight away that she was one of these special windows, for her life revealed to me a God of love and grace. Ana Lisa is a gentle, humble servant of God. She views life and this world through the heart lenses of a loving and forgiving God.

I believe God has given Ana Lisa a number of wonderful gifts, and one of these gifts is the ability to use words to describe the human journey with God. This journey may, at times, be very fragile or complicated. But when life is seen in the context of God choosing to walk with us, then we are able to see the light of God's hope shining through.

This book, *Songs in the Night*, is a wonderful book of poems describing Ana Lisa's journey in a particular year of her life. She shares with the reader her deepest thoughts on that journey through her conversations with a loving God. The poems describe this journey; a journey that is not too different from our own.

I encourage you to read these poems, and I'm sure that you too will be able to engage with your Lord and God and see His hope come shining through into your special journey through life.

God Bless,

Bill Dewar
Senior Pastor
Central Baptist Church
Palmerston North
New Zealand

Introduction

This is a story of a year in poems. Of a God who answers prayer with amazing abundance, who walks with us and lives in us, and who is in all that is around us; and who is always speaking to us as we hold out our pen, or our paint brush, our hands or our lives.

And as I have journalled over this past year, the prayer I whispered in my heart in February 2013, the prayer in which I asked 'to write', was answered by a river, a torrent of words. And these are some of them. Words that for me, an ordinary 43 year old mother, wife and employee, living the ups and downs of an ordinary life, in an ordinary year, have given a new insight, an injection of gratitude, and an awareness of God's authorship and signature in and through everything.

Just as the light marks the day from the night, the seasons of the year define our journey. The circular pattern of birth and death, night and day, winter and summer, losing and keeping. And so this volume of poetry reflects the circle of the 'day' – how in the hard times, the nights of our soul, it's often just the reaching out to someone or something – to friends, to family, to hope, to God that enables us to hold out, hold on to the coming of dawn. And when dawn arrives, casting its light across our vision, only the relief of joy can follow. But even our joy in the good times is tempered with the knowledge that on this side of heaven, pain is part of the package, and night will follow day again, just as surely as winter follows summer.

But there's a sense of hope and peace, a deep contentment, which we may, if we look carefully, find weaving through the fabric of our lives, like sap in the tree or blood in our veins, and despite our struggles and inadequacy, we know that because of its presence, despite the season - the losing and the keeping, the living and the dying, our joys and our suffering, we are —we will always be okay.

Ana Lisa de Jong
October 2014

"My life is a tree, yoke fellow of the earth, pledged by roots too deep for remembrance. To stand hard against the storm. To fill my place. (But high in the branches of my green tree there is a wild bird singing. Wing-free are the wings of my bird; she hath built no mortal nest)"
'THE TREE,' BY KARLE WILSON BAKER (1878-1960)

"Surely your goodness and love will follow me all the days of my life, and I will dwell in the house of the Lord forever."
PSALM 23:6 NIV

Seasons

Seasons are valleys and heights.
Blossoms and ravines, roses and thorns.
Life's river runs still, sometimes storm-shook.

Spring seems like a dream in any other season.
And summer beyond reach in
the falling leaves of autumn, with winter in the breach.

Winter's cold dark passage - is there any other way?
Frozen river, frozen mountain, frozen heart to scale.
Our hope in hibernation, and our faith failing.

Just as summer never lasts, so winter's cold must pass.
It's not over yet - the coldest yet to come,
but we've planted a seed in the midst of our suffering.

We won't know what it will be,
until the pale sun warms earth's crust.
It could be patience, it could be faith, love or simply trust…

A trust in the seasons, that in the summer we bloom,
and in the winter we sow,
without knowing so - the seeds of our joy.

ANA LISA DE JONG

*"The day is yours, and yours also the night;
you established the sun and moon.
It was you who set all the boundaries of the earth;
You made both summer and winter."*

PSALM 74:16-17 NIV

Part 1:
SONGS IN THE NIGHT

"By day the Lord directs his love, at night his song is with me – a prayer to the God of my life."
PSALM 42:8 NIV

There is a Time

Oh Lord, it must first be torn down
before it can be repaired.
For you would turn us and all that is dear,
upside-down, almost beyond repair.
Inside out and torn right through,
until we, with nothing, come to you.

Oh Lord, we must lose what we thought we held,
what we thought to be adhered, as though glued.
You would ask us to release, and let go.
You would ask us to cut away, and expel.
And to let the wounds run clean, under your tender mercy.

Oh Lord, we must grieve what we must lose.
For what we cannot retain, we must lament.
For our carpet that is torn from under us,
we must pine with tears.
Let them fall on the hard, cold ground,
upon which Jesus himself lay - at Gethsemane.

What we once may have spoken,
you whip the words, like the wind, from our mouths.
With anguish you silence us, as we hit the wall.
Render wordless the very prayers and thoughts of our minds.
Until we can only stand in awe, wounded yet still whole,
under the tower of safety - that is your wall.

Where we once would have surrendered for peace,
you would armour us, again, for war.
Against that, which without just fight,
we may lose the ground you have secured.
In the endless battle for our souls,
the balance of power, you would have us restore.

And in this journey called life,
where there is a time for everything under the sun.
In this dance, of love and loss, laughter and mourning.
We must recall that it is all only temporary.
For now we take your hand in the crucifixion,
and then you lead us on to resurrection.

Our lives now, a series of little deaths.
Scattering seeds, as though stones.
So that we may gather, what in sorrow and pain we've sown.
So that our soul may enlarge,
our hope grow and expand as a balloon.
That it might be filled in time, with all of you.

"There is a time for everything, and a season for every activity under the heavens:
a time to be born and a time to die,
a time to plant and a time to uproot,
a time to kill and a time to heal,
a time to tear down and a time to build,
a time to weep and a time to laugh,
a time to mourn and a time to dance,
a time to scatter stones and a time to gather them,
a time to embrace and a time to refrain from embracing,
a time to search and a time to give up,
a time to keep and a time to throw away,
a time to tear and a time to mend,
a time to be silent and a time to speak,
a time to love and a time to hate,
a time for war and a time for peace."

ECCLESIASTES 3:1-8 NIV

The Tender Places

The deeper our need, the further you fill us.
The more we need you, the more you meet us,
at the places most sensitive.

Where we long for you most, we will see you.
When we call out, we will find you there,
even before we take a breath.

We only need to open up, let down our defences.
To you, who longs to hold us close,
in the places where we're loneliest.

Where we have been hurt the deepest,
you would hollow out our hearts.
In the corners that cannot contain you,
until you're done your delicate work.

For you hold the knife and the balm,
you cut and soothe, heal and calm.
As we, both baby and patient, lie in your arms.

For there is no escape from life's hurts,
but there is a remedy, when we are transparent,
and allow your Holy Spirit to touch us,
where we are the tenderest.

*"As a Father has compassion on his children,
so the Lord has compassion on those who fear him…"*
PSALM 103:13 NIV

Sanctification

Break me down,
break me down,
with my tears anoint me.
My pain, let it be the breaking of my will
that leads to the restoration
of my soul.

Your righteousness,
let it be as a robe.
For my tarnished soul, and
faithless heart
cannot face the world,
until I'm clothed in you
and know my true worth.

Lay me down,
lay me down,
low enough to unburden
and lose the weight of my sin.
And lay upon your altar my confession,
my repentance as a holy offering.

Every day, every day,
I'm aware of how I fail you.
Every day, every day,
I'm aware of how you love me.
Every day I must lay, lay it all down,
and you sift through it all, and you shake off the dust

and you replace my crown.

"…who redeems your life from the pit,
and crowns you with love and compassion"
PSALM 133:1 NIV

Brother, Sister

If you could hear my prayers,
if you could know my heart.
If I could hear your prayers
and know your heart.
Would we meet somewhere,
and build a bridge to span the gulf that separates?

If words were found
to clothe our naked pain;
and if our tears could speak
of internal battles, lost and won.
Would we appreciate?
Would we finally understand—to our shame?

If our future hopes
were painted as a picture,
through which God's will
were evidently seen.
Would we see our similarities were greater than our differences?
Would we see that together we share a common dream?

Look into the mirror of each other's hearts.
What you see there simply an image of your own.
Do not look for fault,
or be too quick to condemn.
It's in a glass house that you throw these stones.

A house of glass can't stand too many hits.
We forget whose house we claim to be.
Peacemakers, promised to the precious cornerstone…
But who would blindly bring the building to its knees.

Trust Him with your grievances,
and your broken hopes.
He is strong enough to weather any storm.
But your brother and sister is your keeper.
We turn on one another at our peril.
We turn on ourselves when we condemn.

We will always find what we look for.
So look for what is good, and true and right;
and the light that shines in the darkness,
will not by this present darkness be put out.

Brother, Sister.
Will you hear my earnest prayer?
And come to know how tender is my heart?
I will hear your prayer,
and seek to know you also…
and together we may turn the page
to a whole new start.

*"How good and pleasant it is when God's
people live together in unity!"*
PSALM 133:1 NIV

Missing You

I've gone away, for a while now…
Took my own path,
without a backward glance.
Until I realised, long down the track,
distracted by all that glitters,
that I had left behind the true gold,
and the owner of my heart.

How could I flee from you? Turn around so easily?
Make my focus so narrow,
that even You - the desire for You,
the memory of You,
could grow so pale,
that it would fade into the distance,
in the face of my betrayal.

If I could come to you now, what would I say?
If you could come to me, what would I hear?
If there were nothing between us, what would you do?
Would you run to me, as I would to you?

I've turned away from you, betrayed you,
determined to follow my own selfish will.
Conviction following at my heels,
I blindly sought to obtain
treasures not meant for me;

to fill an empty place,
which really only you can fill.

I cannot even pray.
I cannot find the words to say,
'I am so sorry - don't give up on me'.
Because still I am drawn away.
Have no strength for the fight;
for the battle in my heart, which you alone must wage,
because I, I simply can't.

If I could come to you now, what would you say?
If you could come to me, what would I hear?
If there were nothing between us, what would you do?
Would you run to me, as I, prodigal daughter, must run to you?

"Whether you turn to the right or to the left, your ears will hear a voice behind you, saying, 'This is the way; walk in it'."
ISAIAH 30:21 NIV

Loss

How is the loss to be borne?
By bearing down upon the pain.
Come closer to me Lord.
In every wave of grief come near,
and lay on my tender aching heart, your balm.

How is the loss to be borne?
By your healing touch turning it to gain.
So come with the gift of yourself, Lord.
To fill each corner of my empty heart,
now echoing in mournful refrain.

Let my mourning turn to joy, Lord.
The joy that only comes from your hand.
The mourning which will give way to morning.
As you gently take my heavy cloak,
transform it to a garment of praise.

And as I sing to you my praise Lord,
may it be sweeter for my brush with pain.
Capturing depths that joy alone can't reach.
Stirring the dark corners of my heart,
that my prayers may ring with deeper meaning.

How is the loss to be borne?
By going with it - by being borne upon.
The waves that I fear will take me under,
will only bear me to the next shoreline.
Where tomorrow I may find I can wake,
and face, a new dawn.

"He has sent me to bind up the broken-hearted, to proclaim freedom for the captives and release from darkness for the prisoners, to proclaim the year of the LORD's *favour and the day of vengeance of our God, to comfort all who mourn, and provide for those who grieve in Zion—to bestow on them a crown of beauty instead of ashes, the oil of joy instead of mourning, and a garment of praise instead of a spirit of despair."*

ISAIAH 61:1-3 NIV

God is in a Stone

God is often found in a book,
but it's not the source of Him.
Sometimes the words are insufficient,
and we are only left wanting.

Sometimes God is found in a storm,
and sometimes in a brilliant blue sky.
But often when we look He's not what we seek,
and we turn and pass Him by.

God is often in tears,
when we expect Him in joy.
He doesn't leave when we grieve,
like a guest at the door.

He <u>is</u> in the pain, and by trying to smile,
it's Him we ignore.
He is there in our experience,
perhaps not what we want, but what we need;
and when our heart hurts,
it's deeper in He leads.

God is in a stone, as much as in a flower.
He is depth, as much as He is height.
We do not fail for losing.
No, we gain a blessing in the night.

The value of pain does not make joy less.
No, joy is the crown and the prize.
But it's empty without the knowledge of what it cost,
without pain to measure it by.

***"And we know that in all things God works
for the good of those who love him, who have
been called according to his purpose."***
ROMANS 8:28 NIV

Black and Blue

Oh God....

Black and blue, I come to you.
Bruised and empty,
I pray you'll quench me
of this thirst for you...

Of this thirst for joy -
renewed.
For strength, faith
and hope to flow through;

My barren heart,
like a desert parched,
broken, and
in need of you.

For the well is dry.
And I torn in two,
try to stand,
fruitlessly,
on a foundation
come unglued.

Oh God....

*Where are you?
No words left
to call to you.
I can only silently
trust in your*

endless mercy.

*I can only
parched and thirsty…
plead for rain.
Like the dry and broken land,
suffering without you.*

*But I know
you haven't left me,
and your springs
deep, eternal;*

*will rise up to renew me.
Fill the well
that's empty, thirsty,
with a love that can continue.*

*With a source
that can re-fuel me,
to carry on until
tomorrow.*

Oh God….

*Black and blue, I come to you.
Bruised and empty,
praying you'll
strengthen me.*

*Shaky on a
broken foundation;
still dependent
on your healing.*

*Still grasping
for your hand
to comfort and
enable me.*

*To hold on, and
not relinquish;
a desperate, hope-driven
expectation….
of a different ending.*

*"For he satisfies the thirsty and fills
the hungry with good things."*
PSALM 107:9 NIV

Heartbroken

Heartbroken…

My hopes fading,
falling victim to fears.
Fears that hold up a mirror,
and take my pain and enlarge it to claim
all of the years still ahead.

Heartbroken….

My dreams stolen,
before they've hardly drawn breath.
The way forward, too coloured by the past,
that there seems nothing on which to build,
a new hope, a foundation to last.

So heartbroken…

My optimism is shaken,
taken hostage by doubt.
Until the future I saw as certain to be ours,
fades, until even my faith can't resurrect,
the hopes of my despairing heart.

So heartbroken…

That even your promises
can't seem to shine their light,
into the crevices, the cracks that
will refuse to mend; while the pressure remains,
while the stresses strain, and the darts hit their mark.

God

So heartbroken…

I fail to understand,
that my brokenness is your ministry.
That only your comfort, your tender love,
can heal the parts that need your touch.
Can ensure the past will not corrupt, the future you would have for us.

So God

I place my heart in your hands.

Broken and tender.
Bruised and surrendered.
Subdued in your grasp, so that you may use my tears as balm.
To shore up the cracks, that in you I may be intact,
restored to strength once again - in your embrace.

*"His left arm is under my head, and
his right arm embraces me."*
SONG OF SOLOMON 2:6 NIV

Don't Go Back

Don't go back.
The past has been, to leave a dream
to haunt...

But

Don't go back.
It will never be, as now it seems
again...

It was in its place, that it was best.
In the past, leave it to rest.
Love has many guises.
Today he has a new face.

Leave, leave yesterday.
You can lock the door.
For it can't leave you,

it has been before...

"Whatever is has already been, and what will be has been before…"

ECCLESIASTES 3:15 NIV

The Bright Side

I see a pain in your beautiful eyes;
anger, disappointment, trust betrayed.
I sense a loss of more than pride;
the loss of dreams, that you held close inside.

But I reflect as I look up at the oak tree standing high,
that though your leaves may fall and you stand vulnerable and tired.
Though the wind may rip your limbs,
and your trunk is torn down its very side…

You are to keep holding on, keep standing strong.
For now it's hard, but inevitably, like the turn of the tide,
the seasons change, to brighter days,
so raise your head, and wait - dignified.

My friend – life has a way of restoring itself.
Like a submerged vessel we surface again on our upside.

I see a smile on your beautiful face;
so brave on the surface, but underneath I feel it shake.
Underneath I know that you stand battle-worn;
only held by a sorely tested faith.

But I reflect as I look up at the oak tree alongside.
I think of how we're not meant to hold it all inside.
But we're to lean on our neighbours when we've lost our resolve.
Lean hard in the storm against their strong side.

We're to keep holding on, and standing proud.
We're to look into eyes that reflect our true selves.
And believe that in the end, God's plans will still abide.
If I can give you nothing but my faith in you, take it as true and tried.

For what are friends for, but to wait with us until the dawn?
To show us still, that there's a bright side.

"If either of them falls down, one can help the other up. But pity anyone who falls and has no one to help them up. Also, if two lie down together, they will keep warm. But how can one keep warm alone?"
ECCLESIASTES 4:10-11 NIV

Songs in the Night

There are songs in the night,
which the light of day cannot reach
It takes sorrow of soul to touch that deep.

There is peace of spirit,
which joy cannot bring.
It takes loss to still the heart's constant stirring.

There is humbleness of heart
only gained through pain.
And in earths' broken things, is Christ's greatest gain.

For to be whole in spirit, flesh must be rent.
To be holy within, the will must be bent.
Neither comes except by a fall…

"I will give you a new heart and put a new spirit in you; I will remove from you your heart of stone and give you a heart of flesh."

EZEKIEL 36:26 NIV

Part 2:
ODE TO THE DAWN

"I wait for the Lord, my whole being waits, and in his Word I put my hope."
PSALM 130:5 NIV

To Remember

Open your eyes and the dream slips by.
Too fast to grasp, until there's only now.
Watch the sun rise in the eastern sky.
As the night is left where memories lie.

Forgetting, forgotten – the mind of man,
the heights of knowledge cannot stand.
Even a memory has to fade,
in the rising dawn of a new day.

Our spirits know what our minds cannot fathom.
Their memories aren't their own.
Just like a voice, a song, a scene,
will draw our souls and take us home.

A place where the sun doesn't need to rise.
And memories have no use.
Where God is not a glimpse,
and belief not something we choose.

For the dream is never lost.
It's there again when we close our eyes.
And to be born is only forgetting -
and to die is remembering why.

"And if I go and prepare a place for you, I will come back and take you to be with me that you also may be where I am. You know the way to the place where I am going."

JOHN 14:2-4 NIV

Joy

Joy is in the middle.
Whoever thought joy was at the end -
at the end of our afflictions, trials and suffering -
was wrong. It's right in the centre of things.

Joy takes us by surprise,
when we thought that all was dark.
Joy's in the glow that glints through the curtains drawn,
and leads us to search out the light.

And as joy sits at our feet,
we scan the horizon far.
Looking for an answer, or a reason -
not believing - that peace is ours right now.

Joy is the anchor that holds,
while the sea is churning rough.
While the love runs out - runs cold -
and the vessel's tossed to and fro.

Joy continues to hold.
Its strength made perfect in weakness.
Its grace continuing to absolve us,
of shame, of guilt, of faithlessness.

Joy keeps us fighting, keeps us grasping -
to hope, to a future way.
As a laser that pierces the night sky,
it points out the coming of day.

Yes, joy is in the middle.
Whoever thought joy was at the end;
at the end of our afflictions, trials and suffering -
was wrong. It's right in the centre of things.

"...and not only that, but we also glory in our sufferings..."
ROMANS 5:3 NIV

*If 'Hope is the thing with feathers that perches in the soul',
then too many knocks and trials can tend to make it fall.
And for a moment we can wonder where hope has fled,
when the dark clouds shield the sun, and our dreams die unrealised.*

*When our 'Plan A's' become 'Plan B's' we didn't envisage,
when our optimism is faltering and tears blind our vision.
It's hard to believe that God's plans can't be shaken.
His ways are not our ways – and we won't be forsaken.*

*That even in the valley, we can be safe in His will.
Even in the storm, we can find shelter still.
In the stillness of His presence, where hope resides,
we can renew our strength; and realign ourselves…*

*To a future that may look different to the one we've imagined.
But which we can trust by whose hand it is fashioned.
Though to all appearances it may shatter our dreams,
and break our very hearts, until we recast our vision.*

*If 'hope is the thing with feathers that perches in the soul'
then hope, though it may fall, may yet 'spring eternal'.
And with wings, we have the freedom to take what we're dealt,
and make something new out of what seems set in concrete.*

Make something beautiful out of the present reality,
though it be rough and stormy, and hard to stay steady.
Make something precious out of all the broken pieces.
As in hand with Him we redesign and restore them to completion.

And hope, with love and faith, are closely related.
It's because of our love, that our hope can't be shaken.
It's because of our faith, that our love doesn't weaken.
It's because of our hope, that our faith remains unbroken.

"And now these three remain: faith, hope and love.
1 COR 13:13 NIV

"Hope is the thing with feathers – that perches in the soul – and sings the tune without the words – and never stops – at all."
EMILY DICKENSON (1830-1886)

Love Knocks

Love knocks on my door.
He stands near on soundless feet,
although I hardly know He is there.

Yet it's in my solitude that He accompanies me;
in my loneliness He keeps vigil;
of all my doubts, and fears and struggles, He is aware.

Love knocks so quietly,
waits so patiently,
I almost miss the insistent tone.

Until the echoes reverberate around my empty heart;
my ears prick to an unworldly sound;
and I am drawn to Him as to a siren's song.

Love stands waiting.
While I look for Him in other places,
looking for a love that cannot satisfy.

Not knowing joy was mine for the taking.
Not knowing it was His love I was lacking;
not knowing, until the door I finally open.

Love stands smiling.
No sin too large to dissuade Him,
no temptation too great to supersede Him.

My love simply stands for me;
blessings at his feet won for me.
Joy and peace; contentment, freedom.

How can I refuse Him?

"And those he predestined, he also called; those he called,
he also justified; those he justified, he also glorified."
ROMANS 8:30 NIV

Help me to See

Help me to see.
See what you've given me.
Help me to cherish the days as they are.
Grey or blue, or in-between.
As they come, to cherish them.

Help me to receive.
Receive what you've given me.
To accept all from your hand,
as it arrives with open palm.
Pleasure or pain, my wishes tamed.

Help me to believe.
Believe you have my good at heart.
Trust you to never give
what will hurt irreparably, and only
to give what will serve to further me.

Help me to love.
Help me to love with true agape.
Not for gain, or even certainty;
but only to love for the good of the beloved,
because for me your love is enough.

Help me to rest.
Rest through fear and doubt, and frustration.
Rest through struggle, despair, temptation.
Rest my emotions and my will,
in the one who carries me still.

Help me to hear.
Hear above the din of others.
What you long for me to discover;
that you are speaking to me nigh incessantly,
and your words are love unquestionably.

Help me to submit.
There is peace that flows like a river,
for the one who has given up.
Given up stubborn independence,
to depend on the one who delivers.

Delivers the day,
the minute, the hour;
as a blessing, or a spring-time shower.
Not to harm or hinder or hurt,
but only to nourish the soul's parched earth.

Yet our souls,
they take umbrage,
with the hand that gives.
Too ready to distrust the gift,
for it is packaged as we cannot envisage.

We would return it,
or shape it as we expect it.
We would weigh it, and continually assess it.
Instead of going with the flow of your providence,
trusting that you know what is best for us.

So help me to trust you, Lord Jesus.
To see, to hear, believe.
To rest in you and receive what you've prepared.
To welcome all that's held in your hand today,
knowing that in true love it's made.

**"I have made you and I will carry you. I will
sustain you and I will rescue you."**
ISAIAH 46:4 NIV

My Lord

I am not fit for you, my Lord.

My robes are tattered and torn.
My soul is tarnished with the grime of the world.
My eyes are drawn away from you.
My priorities are wrong.

I am not prepared for you, my Lord.
My heart fails to stay true.
My commitment, it burns and wanes.
And if my love were measured
it would come up short - against you.

But My Love - My Love is calling to me.
Rejoicing over me with song.
He knows my heart, and all about me.
He sees the glory in the dust.
He has loved me all along.

My Love, My Love is calling to me.
Who would we be without your love?
With your touch we learn who we already are.
For you transform clay pots into alabaster jars,
and water into wine.

I am beautiful to you, Lord.
My raiment reflecting your light.
My soul is restored to honour you.
And in response to your love,
you become my delight.

I respond to you, my Lord.
As did Mary of Bethany, perfume poured;
Sister of Lazarus, and friend.
As Mary, the Mother in whom you were formed;
Mary Magdalene, for whom life was restored.

I am ready for you, my Lord,
to stand with your Church, as your Bride.
Yet even now I can be loved by you;
as daughter, sister, disciple,
friend of Christ.

I need not wait until you come in glory.
Your glory came to me.
In the form of a little babe,
who showed us the Father's heart;
and for whom I was made.

"The Lord your God is with you, the Mighty Warrior who saves. He will take great delight in you; in his love he will no longer rebuke you, but will rejoice over you with singing."
ZEPHANIAH 3:17

Because you Love me

You know me, God. You know me through and through.
You know myself better than I know myself.
You know what you're making of me.
You know where you're taking me.
I can rest in you.

You know me, God. You know when I'm near and when I'm far.
You know what makes me stray, and what draws me near.
You know for what I'll fall.
You know what I will stand for.
I can depend on you.

You know me, God. You know my character.
You know where I am lax, and where you need to support.
You know what I lack.
You know for what I ache.
I can trust in you.

You know me, God. You know when I turn to you.
You know when I turn my back, and when I vacillate.
You know when I will waver.
You know when I will falter.
I can turn to you.

For I know you, God. I know you to be faithful.
I know you are all that I am not.
I know that you will shore up the gaps,
with abundant undeserved grace.
I can rest assured.

For I know you, God. I know you to be present.
I know you're here when I am there.
Following thoughts far from you.
And yet you will never depart from me.
Of this I can be certain.

For I know you, God. I know you to be true.
I know you to fight for us.
Even when we see ourselves unworthy.
I know that to you, I'll always be your bride.
And you would have me at your side.

So take me God. Come journey with me.
Although I'll try, I may not always honour you,
with the undivided heart that you deserve.
But I will always love you, trust in you, and depend on you.

I will always turn to you. Return to you. Because you loved me first.

"Let us acknowledge the Lord; let us press on to acknowledge him. As surely as the sun rises, he will appear; he will come to us like the winter rains, like the spring rains that water the earth"

HOSEA 6:3 NIV

I Look for You

I look for you.
I look for you without realising it.
It is always you that I seek.
As I look for you in all whom I love, all whom I meet.

And as another day draws to an end,
where I have gone misunderstood, where I have felt neglect.
I become aware that it is only you,
no-one else, in whose love I can be truly complete.

That without you, like half a heart,
or an empty vessel, I only know a lonely ache.
For there's only one, only one that exists
whose love I can rest in – replete.

So I look for you.
And never find you, or at least only in part.
Each person I meet, imperfect yet
reflecting a portion of your perfect heart.

But they can't fulfil.
They never will – they were never made to.
All I can do is try and grasp
in others, what you mean for me – for us…

*'Relationship' - with the only one
who knows each ebb and flow of my heart.
Who will ever perceive my deepest self;
what brings us together, what keeps us apart.*

*So I look for you.
And I finally find you, but only when I have given up.
When I am ready to lay myself down, appreciate others as they are;
quietened by your love.*

*This side of heaven, between the trees,
there will only ever be discontent, and unfulfilled dreams.
If we try to do it all alone,
without your love to fulfil our deepest needs.*

*Your love that makes up for a multitude;
that mends what is broken, fills the gaps.
That transforms our half hearts into whole;
completes us, and provides all that we lack.*

*I look for you.
And I find you, when I am willing to see,
that everyone is a part of the whole, including me.
That I need everyone, but no 'one' too -
for in the end – its only You.*

"Yet this I call to mind and therefore I have hope: Because of the Lord's great love we are not consumed, for his compassions never fail. They are new every morning; great is your faithfulness. I say to myself, "The Lord is my portion; therefore I will wait for him." The Lord is good to those whose hope is in him, to the one who seeks him; it is good to wait quietly for the salvation of the Lord."

LAMENTATIONS 3:21-26 NIV

I Turn to You

You make all things new.
You, of no shadow or turning.
From me I turn to you.

And you take my wayward, shifting heart,
as though it were a precious vessel,
as though it were your most valuable treasure.

And you draw me, reel me in.
You, oh great fisherman of men,
while I fight the line, and toss and turn.

But you keep reeling.
Not giving up, never retreating,
you keep beckoning,
until there is nothing in-between.

And under the weight of your love
my submission is invoked,
until this world I am able to revoke, once again.

So take my heart, and make it your own,
with no shadow or turning,
retreating or disowning.

As your own precious vessel.
Your valuable treasure.
Entirely, utterly yours alone.

You, who makes all things new.
You, of no shadow or turning.
Help me turn to you.

"God did this so that they would seek him and perhaps reach out for him and find him, though he is not far from any one of us."
ACTS 17:27-28 NIV

Where I Stand

Lord God, take my worries, take my fears.
Take my sorrows and all my tears.
Replace them with your joy and your peace,
so I may lie at rest,
assured as a child on her Father's chest.

Lord, the sun shines again after a passing storm,
and I am reminded that all passes,
except God, and my soul stand sure.
I can take comfort in the transitoriness of all things,
because of your constant, enduring love for me.

Lord, joy so often grows at our feet.
While we so focused on looking ahead,
miss the flowers planted with such loving intent,
to bless us where we stand right now -
in your presence.

Lord, we know that you are the great 'I am'.
And that to find you and your peace we must slow down.
Yes, you precede us and hem us in from behind,
but its where we are right now,
that your blessings are found.

So give me the secret of joy and contentment Lord.
An awareness of you in each breath I breathe.
Racing ahead I must rein myself into submission,
to sit at your feet
and drink deep of your wisdom.

Give me the secret of peace and trust Lord.
Give me the water that sustains me continually.
So I don't seek that which leaves me thirsty.
Show me that water is still when left undisturbed,
that the peace of our soul depends on harnessing our thoughts to you.

So Lord, take my worries and all my fears.
Take my sorrows and all of my tears.
Take the burdens of the years,
the year that has been, the year to come.
Assure me that you have it all in hand, but that most of all…

You wait for me where I stand.
Amen.

"Cast all your anxiety on him because he cares for you."
1 PETER:5-7 NIV

Grace

If grace is indeed a river,
then it has no end;
except where it flows to the ocean,
where still more of it abounds.

Yet, why do I think of it as
something that can run out,
that can be exhausted
at the first real need?

That there is a limit
to its consumption?
That God is not as generous,
as His Holy Word decrees?

While to others,
He is rich in mercy.
His love and compassion
never-ending.

Like the distant horizon, extending…
into forever.

But for me…

For me, there is a limit
to His favour, to His love.
For if He truly understands,
then He can clearly see my heart.

And that is what I am afraid of.
For the love that He has given me,
has made me afraid of disappointing Him
because how can I ever achieve…

The holiness He requires of me.
The righteousness to even come near.
The ability to lift my face,
hold His gaze, and be worthy.

Be worthy of His kindness.
Be worthy of His love.
Be worthy of a river of reprieve,
let alone an ocean.

An ocean…
of never-ending GRACE.

Whoever has been forgiven little
loves little, His Holy word says.
I cannot fail you, or be forsaken by you.
Help me to understand.

It's in our need you meet us.
In our inadequacy, that you are enough.
Our faithlessness that you are true.
Our humanity that you came, our sin that you perished.

*And the holiness He requires of me
was long ago achieved,
by the one whose heart of love for me
once hung upon a tree.*

*If grace is indeed a river,
then it has no end;
except where it flows to the ocean,
where still more of it abounds.*

*And your love and compassion never-ending
has never ended for me.
I can never be separated from you,
despite my unbelief.*

*For your favour and your love
does not depend on what I've done,
or the state of my heart;
but on what you've given.*

*What you have sacrificed
in tears of blood,
blood that has made it possible
for me to be good enough.*

*Lord, I stumble and I fall.
Your way is narrow, but it is life.
Help me to remember when I fall,
it's into the river, the river of grace.*

*Whose streams
'make glad the city of God,
in that holy place
where the most high dwells'.*

*And the river.
The 'river of the water of life,
that flows from the throne of God',
Which without …*

without, we'd be lost.

*"As the deer pants for streams of water, so my soul pants for
you, O God. My soul thirsts for God, for the living God."*
PSALM 42:1-2 NIV

He's Calling

He's calling, beseeching you.
Can you not hear Him?
Calling in the wind's wild pace, and in the wave's tumultuous crash.
Calling right now - calling across centuries.

He's pining, longing for you.
Can you not feel Him?
Pining in the moon's golden glow, pining in the softly falling snow.
Pining for you to reach out your hands, and take His own.

He's falling, fallen for you.
Can you not sense it?
Tender as a friend's close embrace, earnest as a lover's open gaze.
Falling, as far from Him you roam, to lead you home.

He's yearning, burning for you.
Can you not perceive Him?
His lover's heart on full display, in His Holy Word portrayed.
Yearning for communion, He will not rest until the moment of re-union.

Though He might call out for us forever.
Though He might reach for us from heaven.
In truth He has never been far, as close to us as breathing.
And to cross the divide to Him, is simply to reach to Him.
For In Him we live and move, and have our very being.

He's seeking, entreating you.
Will you not recognise Him?
He comes as a brother, as a sister, as a husband.
He comes as the answer to all of your longings.

He's craving, aching for you.
Will you not believe Him?
There has never been, nor will ever be, a love that resembles His.
We wander the world in fruitless searching, to find what we need at home.

He's smiling, desiring you.
Will you not respond to Him?
He would entreat you to assent to Him, conquer you to bless you, and reveal the way to Him is in submission.

Yes he's here, He's here right now.
Will you not receive Him?
He stands at the door of Your heart and knocks.
Come, receive His invitation – for from the beginning, He's sought this union.

"Here I am! I stand at the door and knock. If anyone hears my voice and opens the door, I will come in and eat with that person, and they with me."

REVELATION 3:20 NIV

Your Table

You invite me to your table every day.

I, drawn by the world, would rather gather crumbs
from the floor;
than come and sit,
and know your gaze,
and the blessings you have stored.

Drawn for me, from your storehouse
in heaven,
and laid with love on my plate;
at the place prepared for me since time began,
and which, for me, you will sit, and wait.

And the invitation doesn't lapse.
The meal, it doesn't grow cold.
Though I, drawn by the world,
and my hearts vagaries, and focus on life's ills,
hardly know, what is good.

Yet today I see you waiting,
and today I feel your smile -
and I fall in love a little more
as you draw me, and restore me;
until I can climb up from the floor.

Insistently you draw me,
until boldly I can come.
Face raised towards you,
tears of gratitude falling,
as an anointing on your skin.

Lovingly you call me,
until it's you I can't ignore.
And as I fall into your arms,
from this vantage I can see
what has been laid before me all along.

You invite me to your table
every day.
Whether I come is up to me.
Whether I do, or whether I don't
you simply wait.

And you call....

"But because of his great love for us, God, who is rich in mercy, made us alive with Christ even when we were dead in transgressions— it is by grace you have been saved. And God raised us up with Christ and seated us with him in the heavenly realms in Christ Jesus."

EPHESIANS 2:4-6 NIV

The Edge

I stand in my heels at the edge of the year.
An ocean stretches before me in view.
Although I search the horizon's haze,
I cannot foresee what lies ahead,
and must cast off my shoes.

Tentatively, gingerly, I tip my toes in the year.
The cold surprises and I draw back, preferring the safe and the near.
'Cannot I just stay at the edge?', I ask.
'There's beauty behind and around - who knows what lies ahead,
and I might leave it behind.'

Tenderly, gently, I feel you take hold of my hand.
And assured from your grasp, to the depths of my heart,
I know that you have a plan.
'It's just cold to start,' you say, 'but come venture in,
for I'll never leave you alone'.

So I take a last fleeting look behind,
cherishing all that's been.
Knowing part of what lies ahead, it's backwards
I would prefer to swim.
But with my trust conquering my fear
I find I can take a step in.

Wonder of wonders, its warmth surprising,
I find myself drawn into the sea.
And buoyed by hope, buoyed by joy
I find courage to let go of the familiar shore,
and float in serenity.

The sun casts diamonds of light on the surface around,
and my skin is warmed at its touch.
And in the ocean's embrace, I let go my haste to know it all at once.
As I realise that You are the ocean, You are the year,
and nothing is left to chance.

"…In his love and mercy he redeemed them; he lifted them up and carried them all the days of old."
ISAIAH 63:9 NIV

Part 3:

JOY IN THE MORNING

"..satisfy us in the morning with your unfailing love, that we may sing for joy and be glad all our days."
PSALM 90:14 NIV

Limitless Hope

*With the dawn of each new day
Hope comes; rising with the sun.
He longs that we be open to his touch;
receptive to the one…*

*Who comes on sandaled feet,
with mercies that are new.
A gift that has your name engraved,
the gift of a day held out to you.*

*It is He that wakes and seeks you;
asks you touch, taste and see.
All He's laid before you this day;
to come down on bended knee.*

*Slow down and let your burdens fall.
Breathe and feel your heart rise up.
Every breath a gift, every moment another chance;
for hope, for life.*

*With the dawn of each new day
Healing comes; heralded with the light.
It is His peace that soothes,
and strengthens us with His might.*

To stand and greet the day,
to open our eyes and behold.
That each season has its blessings,
each cloud is lined with gold.

It is He that wakes and seeks you;
bids you follow Him this, and every day.
Come in and fellowship with Him.
He has stored blessings in your name.

The blessing of a future.
And a hope that doesn't fail.
A future assured of His presence,
that begins anew with every day.

"He said to me: "It is done. I am the Alpha and the Omega, the Beginning and the End. To the thirsty I will give water without cost from the spring of the water of life. Those who are victorious will inherit all this, and I will be their God and they will be my children."

REVELATION 21:7 NIV

To the Sun

There is hope for a tree.
If cut down, it buds again at the scent of water.
There is hope for us.
In your tender mercy,
our failings are not fatal,
and our missteps only temporary.
For you steady us when we falter,
and you promise us eternity.

You turn us back toward you,
as a tree grows to the sun.
As its roots search out sustenance
we seek the only one,
who satisfies.
And to whom we lift our face,
to whom we re-affirm our faith,
the author and the giver of all grace.

There is hope for the pot,
that is not responding as it should.
For the potter holds the wheel,
the artist the brush. Just as in art, there's no mistake,
the designer will not rush.
Sometimes with great intent,
he'll re-mould his design,
so that with all creation, he may announce it as 'good'.

So we can believe when he speaks of eternity,
of 'new covenants' that wash us clean.
At the scent of water we can re-bud,
though we may feel dead in the ground.
We can have faith in his goodness and mercy,
that follows us to where-ever we have run.
We can respond as the tree, as the pot.
Let him change us, and turn us to the sun.

"At least there is hope for a tree: If it is cut down, it will sprout again, and its new shoots will not fail. Its roots may grow old in the ground and its stump die in the soil, yet at the scent of water it will bud and put forth shoots like a plant."

JOB 14:7-9 NIV

The Way of the Cross

He has risen.
And His way points straight to heaven.
Now dead-end roads no longer entrap,
nor mountains fail to mar our vision.

For we have seen the highway to heaven.
From tomb to throne, He shines upon
the road alight with His victorious presence.
The road which beckons us home.

He has risen.
And we are invited to follow Him.
As we do our earthly problems grow dim,
when viewed in the light of heaven.

And to us who believe He is a well-spring.
Provision for our daily needs,
and mercy to guarantee an eternity.
The water of life freely given.

He has risen.
And yet without His crucifixion,
would we seek to follow Him?
Would we know what sacrifice means?

But Christ our King has taken His throne.
Christ our friend leads us on.
His grip firm, as he affirms,
the way of the cross leads home.

"Here is my servant, whom I uphold, my chosen one in whom I delight; I will put my Spirit on him, and he will bring justice to the nations. He will not shout or cry out, or raise his voice in the streets. A bruised reed he will not break, and a smouldering wick he will not snuff out. In faithfulness he will bring forth justice; he will not falter or be discouraged till he establishes justice on earth."

ISAIAH 42:1-4 NIV

Christmas Morning

God came to us.
His journey begun as a seed.
The smallest treasure, placed by the mightiest hand;
into the secret place of a daughter of Adam,
that we in good time may receive.

God came to us.
The longest journey,
thousands of years, universes spanned;
waiting for a time ordained, from the time of Eve,
to patiently grow from the smallest seed.

God came to us.
On a donkey's back, in a warm dark womb enveloped.
He came in humility, in vulnerability,
and borne by love enacted in obedience,
He was carried to His destiny, to outwork His mighty plan.

God came to us.
And like a giant apple tree,
hewn from the smallest pip, He grew;
as a babe in need, in total dependence, in Mary's womb.
Until it was our time, our turn, to make Him room.

God came to us.
But there was no room.
The inn was full and not one would let Him in.
As though there were a flaw in His mighty plan,
which may be, if not for the rightness of His humble origins.

For God came to us,
not only as a King, but as a servant.
And only a stable, which opened wide its doors,
could serve as the birthplace of a babe,
who was both King and ransom to us all.

God comes to us still.
In the form of gracious, humble, sacrificial love.
In the form of His precious one and only Son.
The gift of Christmas, that has never stopped giving
since that first wondrous Christmas morn.

"This is how the birth of Jesus Christ came about: His mother Mary was pledged to be married to Joseph, but before they came together, she was found to be with child through the Holy Spirit. Because Joseph her husband was a righteous man and did not want to expose her to public disgrace, he had in mind to divorce her quietly. But after he had considered this, an angel of the Lord appeared to him in a dream and said, "Joseph son of David, do not be afraid to take Mary home as your wife, because what is conceived in her is from the Holy Spirit. She will give birth to a son, and you are to give him the name Jesus, because he will save his people from their sins. "All this took place to fulfil what the Lord had said through the prophet: "The virgin will be with child and will give birth to a son, and they will call him Immanuel"— which means, "God with us." When Joseph woke up, he did what the angel of the Lord had commanded him and took Mary home as his wife. But he had no union with her until she gave birth to a son. And he gave him the name Jesus".

MATTHEW 1:18-25 NIV

No Need

There is no need to worry for me.
I find joy and beauty,
in everything.
All that happens has its purpose.
In everything I derive meaning.

Now as I lie writing on the grass,
I see the hydrangea,
its time has passed.
Its petals once bright, turned to brown.
Its full blown bloom faded now.

Yet at the stem, new life begins.
Leaf as green as
the return of spring.
Nothing is ever truly lost.
Everything in its time is replenished.

Life comes knocking at our door.
Even while on our knees,
no strength to stand tall.
Life quietly
rebuilds and restores.

*As with new sap, the branch re-springs
back into shape,
as it once had been.
So we know that life returns anew,
to transfuse us with joy again.*

*So there is no need to worry for me.
I search for joy in everything.
Even loss I count as gain.*

*The treasure of the past never gone -
only re-framed.*

*"For I will pour water on the thirsty land, and streams on
the dry ground; I will pour out my Spirit on your offspring,
and my blessing on your descendants. They will spring up like
grass in a meadow, like poplar trees by flowing streams."*
ISAIAH 44:1-5 NIV

To Know You

We are made of you.
Each cell infused with mighty life
from an almighty God.

From a seed within,
a plan laid before the dawn of time unfurled.
And we became…

Became a living, breathing
part of you;
parted from you, on this earth.

And as our body grew
our hearts knew
that they did not quite belong…

And yearned for home.
Longing to 'know'
the One for whom we were made.

We are made for you.
Each cell holding a promise
of a life lived in your name.

*Of knowing our Creator,
as Abba Father, the one
in whom we find our place…*

*A place that you
ordained for us,
when you laid the earth.*

*From the moment of
our being, you drew near
and spoke our name.*

*Speaking words of love,
and whispers of assurance,
to draw us home.*

*We were made to be loved.
Willed into being,
destined and claimed.*

*Nothing random about us.
No mistake or accidental
chance – but planned.*

*Our life, no matter
how small or insignificant to us,
of great meaning to Him.*

We - called into being,
By God the Father,
who longed for still another…

Child to love.
To image him with
the unique beauty that could only belong

to a creation of God.

"Everyone who is called by my name,
whom I created for my glory,
whom I formed and made."
ISAIAH 43:7 NIV

There is an Ocean

We, so small and plain
and self-contained,
we live lives full of
petty concerns, and selfish gain.

We, all wound up and tight
and self-absorbed,
we draw up the drawbridge,
and pull shut the door.

With our concern for self
we become confined,
we narrow our world,
until there's only room for one.

With our focus drawn in
we are cut off from Him,
the source of our joy, our power,
our love, our very fulfilment.

Open wide, open up.
There is an ocean at your door.
There is a river that through you would flow.
Behind you is the author of it all.

His is the strength that propels,
His the love that heals,
His the song that delights our heart,
His the touch that soothes.

His the deep contentment,
His the answer to our questions,
His the almighty provision,
His the balm to our wounds.

As heaven is high, and the earth is wide
so we can uncoil;
grow up like a seedling to the sun,
and in his warmth feel our hearts thaw.

We, so small and plain,
and self-contained.
We, who live lives of fruitless striving,
and senseless pain.

We, all wound up and tight
and self-absorbed;
we can open to his touch,
fling wide the door.

And as we do so, we can breathe.
Now what others think no longer matters.
Our fears haven't power to haunt,
our illusions shatter.

Sons and daughters of a higher power,
adopted in his Kingdom;
we finally sense from whom we've come,
whose love is entwined through every living thing.

We can reach out and connect,
without plans or agendas.
We can in freedom relate and trust,
and to His will we surrender.

We can love and be loved,
and as bearers of his light;
we can know the beauty of giving and receiving,
for naught but His delight.

Open wide, open up.
There is an ocean at your door.
There is a river that through you would flow.
Behind you is the author of it all.

"Can you fathom the mysteries of God? Can you probe the limits of the Almighty? They are higher than the heavens above—what can you do? They are deeper than the depths below—what can you know? Their measure is longer than the earth and wider than the sea"

JOB 11:7-9 NIV

Something to Show You

'I've got something to show you.
Turn your eye inward,
for it's not found without.
Magnify me, shine a light within,
for my Word is written on your heart.'

'I've got something to share with you.
Take time for me.
Others will come and they will go,
tenuous connections made at best;
but my presence is eternal.'

'I've got something to teach you.
Life's lessons lead to me.
My revelations are found in communion.
Come withdraw;
and resist your own way.'

'I've got something to give you.
Something the world can't provide.
Why do you seek what will leave you empty?
My desire is to love you.
Fulfil what can't be satisfied.'

'I've got something for you.
Something to tame your restless will.
A thirst for me; a bond with me,
a relationship,
no other can come near to.'

'I've got something promised for you.
Which no moth or thief can destroy.
Life enriched by the knowledge of my eternal love;
As my heart beats,
my breath breathes, with you forevermore.'

"Come to me, all you who are weary and burdened, and I will give you rest. Take my yoke upon you and learn from me, for I am gentle and humble in heart, and you will find rest for your souls. For my yoke is easy and my burden is light."
MATTHEW 11:28-30 NIV

The Way

Jesus, our way to the Father,
a path alight with His love.
Paved with unconditional acceptance,
inlaid with promises from above.

Come walk the way to the Father.
The journey, though it's not far at all,
asks of us trust and vulnerability.
It needs us to open a door.

A door to the heart's own centre.
A place He would dwell within.
The way doesn't lead beyond us, to Heaven.
The way is always deeper in.

Jesus, our way to the Father,
He walks the path with us.
As Father, Son and Holy Spirit,
He's our guide, our path, and our residence.

It is not far to the Father above,
Jesus, with His blood, has made a way.
For you to not only be acceptable - but adored,
the apple of your Father's eye.

Jesus, our way to the Father.
Let the truth open your eyes to Him,
and as the Holy Spirit indwells you,
believe that - "I am His and He is mine".

"Jesus replied, 'Anyone who loves me will obey my teaching. My Father will love them, and we will come to them and make our home with them'."
JOHN 14:23 NIV

God in Me

God of the storm
is living in me…

The infinite power,
all consuming, overwhelming.
A furnace of energy where the
thunder is stored,
and where the lightening is born,
resides in me?

Creator

Who makes moons that draw oceans,
stars to navigate by.
Whose vastness who can comprehend,
whose footstool is the sky,
is contained by me?

Father

Who gave His only Son.
Love that can only be measured by His suffering.
Hanging on the cross,
the cross 'between the trees',
dying for me…..

So that He might be resurrected, so that I might be redeemed,
that He would dwell in me?

Oh Great God

Who encloses and indwells me,
with the heartbeat of the blessed Trinity.
Whose river of living water
arises from eternity.

Never let me forget the truth of your presence.
For he who seeks you only without
fails to know the rivers of delight,
which flow from our innermost selves.

Oh Great God

Consume me, fill and transform me.
Not only with head knowledge,
but with a heart forever bonded
in relationship, in union with

You – Father, Holy Spirit,

Son of God.

"Before long, the world will not see me anymore, but you will see me. Because I live, you also will live. On that day you will realize that I am in my Father, and you are in me, and I am in you."

JOHN 14:19-20 NIV

Learning of Love

If life is not to learn 'of' love,
then what is it for?
If life is not for love to be born in us,
then what then is our purpose?

Yet, in life, we grow, believing we must learn 'how' to love.
That love were a skill to gain,
to better and perfect,
until we have finally obtained…

righteousness and worthiness to bear His name.

Yet what if love were in a name?
His holy name.
And this love, that is being made perfect in us,
were His love: rather than our own.

What if His love were for us 'first'?
And what if the key
to learn to love
was to, in His love – immerse?

Rather than to attain…

What if life were to learn to believe?
To take Him at his word.
That God is love, that we are loved,
and as His children - cherished, adored.

That to lift our heads in the face of such love,
is to be encouraged, renewed, restored…
To our place in Christ,
that our Father would have us fill,

and that Jesus calls us to.

No need for works to reach this place.
Faith makes a way.
Jesus said, "it is finished";
and love fulfilled the law.

Love becomes the consequence of our faith,
a gift from God to an open heart.
Love becomes a way of living,
as it's the language of His grace…

and reveals in us, His light.

And it is our certainty of His love
that teaches us courage, hope and trust.
It is the deepening knowledge of His love
that draws us to love him, and others.

It is the glory of the risen Christ
reflected in our life:
whose face we gaze upon,
and thereby grow in likeness, to love…

with the love,

in which we first were loved.

"Greater love has no one than this: to lay down one's life for one's friends."
JOHN 15:13 NIV

God's Guidance

God's guidance, as gentle as,
the nudge of the rein to a horse that's willing.
Yet without our will in tune with Him,
we carry on blind, impaired of our vision.

Without our eyes on Him, as he leads,
we charge to the front, as though we had foresight to see;
all the lay of the land,
that we're never meant to perceive.

For the knowledge and the wisdom rests in Him.
With our intelligence, all our education,
we cannot even begin -
to navigate our way, to seek to untangle the string;

Of all the choices, all the feelings,
all the myriad of motives and opinions;
that have brought us to where we are today,
wholly dependent on Him to highlight our way.

Lost but found, poor but rich,
reminded of our need to submit.
Reminded of our need to draw into line -
so that we can be guided, rather than blindly lead from behind.

God's guidance, as gentle as,
the pull of the bit to a horse that's willing.
It only knows what its master deems to reveal.
His way made clear to us, only as we yield.

"As the eyes of slaves look to the hand of their master,
as the eyes of a female slave look to the hand of her
mistress, so our eyes look to the Lord our God."
PSALM 123:2 NIV

What Moves You?

Is it only me - that is moved by the sounds of the sea?
Or can hear a thousand sighs in the branches of a tree.
Of winds that have been, of storms and sun-lit leaves?

I can feel the ocean breathing, if I close my eyes.
The rhythm of the ocean has its echoes in my mind.
The song soothes my soul, and its movement is my balm.

What do you feel with a hill and a view?
Do you look for wings locked deep inside you?
Do you ask a question, shed a tear, or make a poem…
Or do you just see an ocean?

I want you to see what I see.
Or if not, for you to show me what you perceive.
My journey isn't yours, and the source of our joy,
is both a lock between us, and a key…

"The heavens declare the glory of God; the skies proclaim the work of his hands. Day after day they pour forth speech; night after night they reveal knowledge. They have no speech, they use no words; no sound is heard from them. Yet their voice goes out into all the earth, their words to the ends of the world."

PSALM 19:1-4 NIV

Surrounded by Love

Can we capture the love of God
as a smile is caught on camera?

Can we capture the light of God
as a moth is confined in a jam jar?

Can we capture the flood of his great mercy,
or rein in the fullness of His grace?

No more than we can draw boundary lines around an ocean,
or stop a river in full pace.

As healing water, He rushes over us.
Only to then run out through our hands.

As the last sun's rays on a summer's day
His warmth is too fleeting to contain.

But His mercies are new every morning.
His boundless love, it knows no end.

He who is thirsty will be satisfied.
He who is hungry need not hunger again.

What can be held, can be measured.
Its height and circumference known.

God is love but he is mystery.
A power that we cannot fully comprehend.

We long for him and he comes.
'As surely as the coming of dawn or the rain of early spring'.

But our human hearts are too imperfect to hold Him.
Our feelings too human to discern the divine.

Can we capture the love of God?
Can we contain Him in all His might?

No, but he has promised to bind us to him,
betrothed with chains of righteousness held tight.

Can we capture the light of God?
Can we bask forever under his warm rays?

No, but weeping may go on for a night,
and joy is as sure as the coming of the new day.

We cannot hold Him; but still close to Him we are held.
We cannot love Him as he deserves, but it was He who loved us first.

We cannot chain Him in, but in chains of love we are bound.
We cannot bind the infinite God,

but it is us that He surrounds.

"In the beginning was the Word, and the Word was with God, and the Word was God. He was with God in the beginning. Through him all things were made; without him nothing was made that has been made. In him was life, and that life was the light of all mankind. The light shines in the darkness, and the darkness has not overcome it."

JOHN 1:1-5 NIV

I See You

I see

*your signature written in a sunset sky,
in soft shades of pink and gold.*

I see

*your reflection cast in the still river,
among the sunlit leaves, and green trees of old.*

And it's your smile…

*I feel when I close my eyes.
The grass under my hands, above me endless sky.*

Your smile

*I know when I stand high
on a hill, with the whole of forever in my view.*

Your voice

*I hear when the Tui sings.
Praising creation, among the blossoms of spring.*

Your voice

*which soothes me in the song
of the sea, as the ocean meets the lonely shore.*

And it's your touch...

*that stirs my soul, warms my heart,
and woos me to the core.*

Your touch

*which I feel through every sense,
as I perceive the gift of this earth.*

Take in the wonder of it all.

**"The heavens proclaim his righteousness,
and all peoples see his glory."**
PSALM 97:6 NIV

He Loves Us

He loves us in the rose's generous bloom,
her petals laid full open to our view.
He loves us in the wind's silent caress,
gentle breeze soft upon our cheek.

He loves us in the sky's brilliant blue,
the promise of a new sunlit day.
He loves us in the sunsets gilt-edged hue,
as a tender token at end of play.

He loves us in the night-time sky,
each star signalling to us in silent entreat;
Of a love, which burns in His heart-sick heart, and
with each turn of the earth, never ceases to beat.

Passion restrained with a gentlemen's honour,
He loves us far more than we can perceive.
His jealous attentions showered upon us,
and yet the fullness of His love we could never receive.

He loves you each day that you open your eyes.
His gift of life another chance for Him,
to woo you in a thousand ways,
until all you can do in response is come.

*Come, to know your needs satisfied, and
on His altar have all your yearnings laid.
Come, to know your dreams fulfilled,
to walk with Him for the length of your days.*

*So come to Him as to the marriage bed.
He wants you heart, body and soul – nothing spared.
We are His Bride, and at His side He would have us stand, so come
to Him – He has 'your' place prepared.*

*He loves you in the rose's generous bloom,
her petals laid full open to your view.
He loves you in the wind's silent caress,
gentle breeze soft upon your cheek.*

*He loves you in the sky's brilliant blue,
the promise of a new sunlit day.
He loves you in the sunsets gilt-edged hue,
as a tender token at end of play.*

*He loves you in the night-time sky,
each star signalling to you in silent entreat;
Of a love which burns in His heart-sick heart, and
with each turn of the earth, never ceases to beat.*

"Therefore I am now going to allure her; I will lead her into the wilderness and speak tenderly to her."

HOSEA 2:14 NIV

Life – As a Gift

If life is indeed a gift,
then we, being alive, must bear the gifts of life.

Our whole and entire purpose…
to breathe it in,
to grow in its nourishment,
to reproduce it, to extend it.
It was given to BE PASSED ON.

Fishes and loaves to feed thousands,
dandelion seeds aloft on the wind.
To land where they will,
and take root where they can,
and bring and give new life.

If life is a gift
then we, the receivers of such a gift;
unwrap it to find
a gift, within a gift, within a gift.
And at the centre – a seed.

A seed, not to be stored
not to be hidden,
not to be discounted,
or disregarded.

But to be planted,
nurtured, encouraged;
cultivated to full and beautiful expression.
And in its strong and tender growth
harvested and released....

Released to grow another harvest.
Released to inspire another gift.
Released to encourage another's faith.
Released to embolden another believer...
to take their seed out of the dark.

We pour it out, until we are empty.
But we refill with each and every breath
of the Holy Spirit;
who is not only the giver of gifts,
but the one and only greatest gift.

In whom is truth, and light and 'fullness' of life.
His fullness flowing into us, that we might release it.
A gift given that we might re-gift it.
Life given for us to respond to Him,
with the gift of our life.

All the tentative talents and fledging abilities,
within that gift of life, harnessed and then
passed on, shared out,
given back, in order that they might flourish...
for His purposes.

"The desert and the parched land will be glad; the wilderness will rejoice and blossom. Like the crocus, it will burst into bloom; it will rejoice greatly and shout for joy. The glory of Lebanon will be given to it, the splendour of Carmel and Sharon; they will see the glory of the Lord, the splendour of our God."

ISAIAH 35:1-2 NIV

What We Believe

With heaven as His throne
and the earth His footstool;
how do we reach, to touch
the hem of His robe?

If we are but dust
and He the Creator;
how do we look at Him?
How low must we bow?

With heaven so far, and
our own life and death
unconceivable;
how do we know…
what we believe?

But He, the very one
who planted the stars
says,
"I did it all for you
so that you would come…

*Come and believe
that I'm not only real
but I am so near
you could reach out and feel…*

*Not just the hem
of my robe but
the scars on my palm.
The very palm
that planted the stars".*

*With heaven as His throne
and the earth His footstool;
He reigns on high
with both might and victory.*

*Yet with our heart His home
and our home in His heart;
we reign with Him
and shall for eternity.*

*As dust we are born,
and as the earth wears down,
we too, are worn down,
by time.*

*But His signature
is on each and every cell;
and life and death's mystery
is that we are eternal.*

*Reborn to know in our heart
what was once unconceivable;
and to grasp the truth
of what was once unbelievable.*

**"To the one who is victorious and does my will to
the end, I will give authority over the nations…
just as I have received authority from my Father.
I will also give that one the morning star."**
REVELATION 2:26-28 NIV

Time, in its relentless surge,
moves on.
Pulling in its wake,
our memories, as the tide.

Heavy, crashing on our hearts,
like it were yesterday.
Then retreating with only the ache of loss
remaining.

Time - we can't catch up.
Full-flight ahead, not fast enough,
touching only the tails of the wind,
left behind.

By time's rush - to where?
Where will it end, the gaining, and the losing?
At the beginning, maybe -
like a circle, like the tide.

"He has made everything beautiful in its time. He has also set eternity in the human heart; yet no one can fathom what God has done from beginning to end."

ECCLESIASTES 3:11 NIV

"Our birth is but a sleep and a forgetting: The Soul that rises with us, our life's star, hath had elsewhere its setting, and cometh from afar: Not in entire forgetfulness, and not in utter nakedness, but trailing clouds of glory do we come."
WILLIAM WORDSWORTH (1770-1850)

Photo Appendix

Cover Photo: Taylor's Mistake, Christchurch New Zealand

Seasons Photo: Wellington Botanical Gardens, Wellington, New Zealand

There is a Time Photo: Russell Waterfront, Bay of Islands, New Zealand

The Tender Places Photo: Wentworth Valley, Whangamata, Coromandel, New Zealand

Sanctification Photo: Mangawhai Heads, Northland, New Zealand

Brother, Sister Photo: Mahurangi Regional Park, Auckland, New Zealand

Missing You Photo: Mahurangi Regional Park, Auckland, New Zealand

Loss Photo: Puriri Bay, Whangaruru North, Northland, New Zealand

God is in a Stone Photo: Stony Bay, Coromandel, New Zealand

Black and Blue Photo: Wairere Boulder Valley, Northland, New Zealand

Heartbroken Photo: Bethells Beach, Waitakere, Auckland, New Zealand

Don't Go Back Photo: Tutukaka Harbour, Ngunguru, Northland, New Zealand

The Bright Side Photo: St Mark's Chapel, RNZAF Base Ohakea, New Zealand

Songs in the Night Photo: Gethsemane Gardens, Christchurch, New Zealand

To Remember Photo: Surfers Paradise Beach, Gold Coast, Australia

Joy Photo: Elliott Bay, Northland, New Zealand

Hope Photo: Puriri Bay, Whangaruru North, Northland, New Zealand

Love Knocks Photo: Goat Island, Leigh, Matakana Coast, New Zealand

Help Me to See Photo: Omapere, Hokianga Harbour, Northland, New Zealand

My Lord Photo: Milford Sound, Fiordland National Park, New Zealand

Because You Love Me Photo: Pararaunui Point, Whangaruru North, Northland, New Zealand

I Look for You Photo: Taylor's Mistake Beach, Christchurch, New Zealand

I Turn to You Photo: Bethells Beach, Waitakere, Auckland, New Zealand

Where I Stand Photo: Mahurangi Regional Park, Auckland, New Zealand.

Grace Photo: Whangamata Surf Beach, Coromandel, New Zealand

He's Calling Photo: Bethells Beach, Waitakere, Auckland, New Zealand

Your Table Photo: Omapere, Hokianga Harbour, Auckland, New Zealand

The Edge Photo: Cook Straight, South Island, New Zealand

Limitless Hope Photo: Motuihe Island, Hauraki Gulf, Auckland, New Zealand

To the Sun Photo: Surfer's Paradise Beach, Gold Coast, Australia

The Way of the Cross Photo: Taylor's Mistake, Christchurch, New Zealand

Christmas Morning Photo: Marlborough Sounds, South Island, New Zealand

No Need Photo: Elliott Bay, Northland, New Zealand

To Know You Photo: Omaha Beach, Matakana Coast, New Zealand

There is an Ocean Photo: Waikawau Bay, Coromandel, New Zealand

Something to Show You Photo: Bethells Beach, Auckland, New Zealand

The Way Photo: Taylors Mistake, Christchurch, New Zealand

God in Me Photo: Pakiri Beach, North Auckland, New Zealand

Learning of Love Photo: Kaipara Harbour, Auckland, New Zealand

God's Guidance Photo: Pararaunui Point, Whangaruru North, Northland, New Zealand

What Moves You Photo: Waikawau Bay, Coromandel, New Zealand

Surrounded by Love Photo: Taylor's Mistake Beach, Christchurch, New Zealand

I See You Photo: Stony Bay, Coromandel, New Zealand

He Loves Us Photo: Whangaruru North, Northland, New Zealand

Life as a Gift Photo: Snell's Beach, Warkworth, New Zealand

What We Believe Photo: Omapere, Hokianga Harbour, Northland, New Zealand

Time Photo: Tawharanui, Warkworth, Auckand, New Zealand

Last Page Photo: Bethells Beach, Waitakere, New Zealand

All photos are the Author's own.

Acknowledgements

"The Tree" by Karle Wilson Baker is reprinted from *Blue Smoke*. New Haven: Yale University Press, 1919.

"The Ode: Intimations of Immortality from Recollections of Early Childhood" by William Wordsworth, is reprinted from *The Oxford Book of English Verse*. Arthur Quiller-Couch, 1919.

"Hope is the thing with feathers" by Emily Dickenson, is reprinted from *The Poems of Emily Dickinson*. Edited by R.W. Franklin, Harvard University Press, 1999.

www.ingramcontent.com/pod-product-compliance
Lightning Source LLC
Chambersburg PA
CBHW042330150426
43194CB00001B/2